Original title:
Mastering Relationship Dynamics

Copyright © 2024 Swan Charm

Author: Kaido Väinamäe

ISBN HARDBACK: 978-9916-89-091-2
ISBN PAPERBACK: 978-9916-89-092-9
ISBN EBOOK: 978-9916-89-093-6

The Journey of Together

Through winding paths we step, side by side,
In laughter and tears, our hearts opened wide.
With every challenge, we learn to adapt,
Navigating life, our hands tightly wrapped.

Mountains may rise, and rivers run cold,
But with you beside me, my fears turn to gold.
Each sunrise brings hope, each sunset a dream,
Together we shine, a united beam.

Pages of Partnership

In the book of our lives, each page we inscribe,
Words of connection, our spirits collide.
Turning the moments, both bitter and sweet,
Creating a story, two hearts that beat.

Chapters unfold with laughter and grace,
Illustrating memories, no time can erase.
In silence we linger, in whispers we share,
Bound by our journey, a love beyond compare.

The Flame of Understanding

A flickering flame that lights up the night,
In shadows, it dances, a beacon of light.
With patience and kindness, we nurture its glow,
Through trials and triumphs, our bond continues to grow.

In moments of silence, we grasp what is true,
The warmth of your heart is a shelter for me too.
In understanding's embrace, we find our way home,
Together forever, no longer alone.

Ebb and Flow

Like waves that pour forth and retreat from the shore,
Our love has a rhythm, an ever-changing core.
In stillness we linger, in motion we find,
The pulse of our journey, closely entwined.

Sometimes we clash like the storm on the sea,
Yet in softest moments, we find harmony.
Embracing the cycles, we dance in the tide,
In ebb and in flow, together we glide.

Companions at Crossroads

On this path we stand, unsure,
Choices lie before our feet.
Hand in hand, we will endure,
Together, our hearts beat.

Voices whisper in the night,
Guiding us through shadow's veil.
With each step, we seek the light,
In silence, our dreams unveil.

Memories woven, threads of gold,
Stories shared, laughter's embrace.
In this moment, brave and bold,
We'll find our truest place.

Futures stretch like open skies,
Horizon beckons us to roam.
With steadfast hearts, we will rise,
In this journey, we find home.

Crossroads may twist and turn,
Yet, side by side, we will choose.
Through the trials, we will learn,
In each other, we can't lose.

The Journey to Us

Step by step, we walk as one,
Every heartbeat draws us near.
Chasing dreams beneath the sun,
With each glance, our vision clear.

Through the valleys, high and low,
Every mountain, we will climb.
In this dance, our souls will flow,
Time dissolves, we lose all rhyme.

Echoes of laughter fill the air,
Paths entwined, no end in sight.
With each story, love lays bare,
Guided by the stars at night.

Seasons change, yet we remain,
Through the storms, we'll find our way.
In our hearts, we'll hold no pain,
For together, come what may.

At the journey's end, we'll see,
A tapestry that us defines.
In this bond, we will be free,
Forever, your hand in mine.

Dance of Entwined Hearts

In the moon's soft, silver glow,
Two souls sway, lost in the night.
Harmony in every throe,
In our hearts, pure delight.

With each step, we move as one,
Gravity pulls us with its charm.
Under stars, our rhythms spun,
In this moment, safe and warm.

Flames ignite with every glance,
A spark ignites the still of air.
Lost within this whispered dance,
Time stands still, without a care.

Whirling dreams, a gentle song,
In this circle, we are found.
Together, where we belong,
Love's sweet echo, profound.

As dawn breaks, we'll hold so tight,
Fingers clasped, forever near.
In each heartbeat, pure delight,
Entwined hearts, we have no fear.

The Art of Connection

In the silence, words take flight,
Eyes that spark, a knowing glance.
Threads of fate, woven so tight,
In this moment, we find chance.

Through the chaos, find the peace,
Every heartbeat syncs in time.
In its beauty, love's release,
Crafting verses, simple rhyme.

Hands that reach across the space,
Touching souls, igniting flames.
In this dance, we find our place,
Guardian of our shared claims.

Bridges built from soul to soul,
A tapestry of hopes unfurled.
In each connection, we are whole,
In this truth, our dreams are swirled.

Let us cherish every thread,
In our hearts, the stories seen.
The art of love, in silence, spread,
Together always, we are keen.

The Map of Us

In the quiet twilight, we sketch our dreams,
Paths entwined, like flowing streams.
Each corner turned, a story unfolds,
Navigating hearts, through whispers untold.

Together we travel, hand in hand,
Marking the moments, each grain of sand.
In laughter and tears, we map the way,
Creating our journey, day by day.

With every detour, we learn and grow,
In the landscape of us, love's gentle glow.
Exploring the shadows, igniting the light,
In the vastness of night, our stars shining bright.

Seasons of Connection

Spring brings laughter, blooms in the air,
New beginnings blossom, tender and rare.
Summer's embrace, warm sun on our skin,
Together we dance, where the joy begins.

Autumn whispers change, leaves falling down,
In the tapestry woven, wearing love's crown.
Winter's chill wraps us in quiet grace,
In the heart's fire, we find our place.

Every season teaches, in its own way,
Connection deepens with each passing day.
Through all the transitions, our bond will grow,
In the garden of time, love's seeds we sow.

Unitas in Diversity

In a world of colors, we stand side by side,
Distinct yet united, in whom we confide.
Every voice cherished, a song in the night,
Harmony rises, a beautiful sight.

Cultures entwined, like vines on the wall,
Learning from differences, answering the call.
Together we flourish, in gardens so vast,
Creating a future, where shadows are cast.

With hearts open wide, we share and explore,
Finding the treasures, hidden in lore.
In unity's warmth, we bloom and we thrive,
Celebrating the beauty in being alive.

The Puzzle of Intimacy

Each piece whispers secrets, a delicate trace,
In the quiet moments, we find our place.
With laughter and silence, our hearts interlock,
Building the depths on a sturdy foundation rock.

Fragments of stories, woven in trust,
In the tapestry of us, a bond that is just.
Every glance shared, a silent embrace,
In the puzzle of life, we carve out our space.

Layer by layer, vulnerability taught,
In the colors of love, a masterpiece sought.
Through storms and sunshine, hand in hand we stand,
Completing the picture, together we've planned.

Choreography of Souls

In quiet dances, hearts align,
Whispers of dreams, twirling in time.
Every step a story unfolds,
In the rhythm of life, love beholds.

Underneath the moon's soft glow,
Bodies swaying, letting hearts show.
A tapestry woven, thread by thread,
In the silent trust where words are led.

Echoes of laughter, shadows play,
Boundless connection in night and day.
Choreographed joys, sorrows impart,
A ballet of souls, a dance of the heart.

The Compass of Empathy

With gentle eyes, the world we see,
A compass guiding, setting hearts free.
Navigating paths of joy and pain,
With understanding, we lose, we gain.

In every story, a lesson waits,
Empathy unlocks the deepest gates.
Through shadows cast, a light we share,
In silence spoken, love fills the air.

The map of kindness stretches wide,
In our hearts, compassion resides.
Letting others' burdens intertwine,
The compass turns, our destinies align.

Tides of Togetherness

Waves rise and fall, a rhythmic dance,
In the ocean of moments, we take a chance.
Together we sail, hearts open wide,
On tides of togetherness, we ride.

The horizon beckons, a promise so bright,
With hands clasped tight, we embrace the night.
In storms we find shelter, under shared skies,
Our spirits entwined, like stars, we will rise.

In anchoring love, we drift and flow,
Through valleys of sorrow, in laughter we glow.
United as one, in the ebb and the flow,
Tides of togetherness, forever we'll know.

The Alchemy of Bonds

Transforming moments, we ignite the spark,
In the alchemy of bonds, we leave our mark.
Forging connections, both rare and true,
In each heartfelt glance, a world anew.

From silver linings to shadows cast,
We weave our stories, the present and past.
Together we sculpt, with love as the tool,
In the hearth of our hearts, we make life the rule.

A mixture of laughter, tears, and grace,
In the cauldron of life, we find our place.
The alchemy of bonds, a treasure for all,
In unity's gold, we rise and we fall.

Unfolding Together

In the quiet dawn, we rise,
With whispers of dreams in our eyes.
Hands entwined, we gently sway,
Together, we'll find our way.

Every laugh, a gentle breeze,
Carving paths through swaying trees.
Side by side, through joy and strife,
Unfolding the beauty of life.

In the garden where we play,
Love's blooms brightening the day.
With every step, a dance so sweet,
Harmony in hearts that meet.

As shadows stretch across the land,
We'll trace our dreams, hand in hand.
In the tapestry of our days,
Unfolding together, through all maze.

The sun sets low, colors blend,
Reflecting love that will not end.
In the twilight, soft and slow,
Together, in dreams, we will glow.

Heartbeats in Synchrony

Two souls entwined, a rhythm flows,
In every heartbeat, love bestows.
Through silent nights and brightened days,
In synchrony, our hearts will blaze.

Like whispered winds that softly sigh,
We share our secrets, you and I.
A dance of echoes in the night,
Guided by stars, our only light.

With every pulse, the world aligns,
In tender glances, love defines.
Together, we rise, unafraid,
In heartbeats' warmth, the doubts are swayed.

As seasons change, and time will pass,
Our love, a mirror made of glass.
Reflecting moments, both small and grand,
In perfect synchrony, we stand.

When silence falls, and shadows creep,
In heartbeats soft, our promises keep.
For in this union, we are found,
Together, forever, love unbound.

The Poetry of Compromise

In whispered words, we forge the way,
With every choice, a chance to sway.
Hearts in balance, a delicate dance,
In compromise, we find romance.

Through stormy skies and sunny beams,
We chase each other's tender dreams.
With open minds, we pave the road,
In the art of love, a shared code.

Each gentle word, a bridge we build,
In every silence, our hearts are filled.
With every step, we learn to see,
The beauty in our differences, free.

When paths diverge, we find a tune,
Together, mornings, nights, and noon.
In the poetry of give and take,
A masterpiece, in love we make.

So let us write with every breath,
The lines of life, beyond all death.
In verses bound by trust and grace,
Compromise carries us, interlaced.

Colors of Affection

In shades of blue, our laughter soars,
With every hue, love gently pours.
Golden rays and emerald dreams,
Painting life in vibrant themes.

Crimson hearts that deeply beat,
In every color, our souls meet.
With every look, and soft embrace,
The palette of love we will trace.

In twilight's glow, soft pastels rise,
Underneath the painted skies.
With whispers of lavender night,
Colors merge, creating light.

Through all the storms, and sunny days,
Our love, a canvas that always stays.
With every stroke, we redefine,
The art of us, both yours and mine.

So let us blend, as colors do,
With every moment, bright and true.
In a world alive with affection's art,
Together, we paint from the heart.

Growing Together

In the garden of time, we sow,
Nurturing dreams as they grow.
Hand in hand, through sun and rain,
We flourish together, joy in the pain.

Roots intertwine, strong and deep,
Harvesting memories, secrets we keep.
Through seasons change, our bond stays true,
A tapestry woven of me and you.

With every challenge, we rise anew,
In laughter and love, our hearts break through.
Together we build, together we strive,
In the growth of our souls, we feel alive.

Time whispers softly in the breeze,
Embracing the moments, our hearts at ease.
In this dance of life, we find our place,
Growing together, time won't erase.

Trust is the soil, love is the rain,
In the garden of us, there's no room for pain.
We bloom in colors, vibrant and bold,
Growing together, our story unfolds.

The Compass of Affection

In shadows cast by moonlight glow,
Our hearts stirred with the ebb and flow.
Held by a compass that points to love,
Guided by stars from the heavens above.

Through winding paths and endless roads,
We share the burden, lighten the loads.
With every heartbeat, a gentle sign,
In the map of affection, your hand in mine.

Fierce as a storm, gentle like rain,
Together we'll navigate joy and pain.
With every compass, our direction is clear,
In the warmth of your smile, there's naught to fear.

Across the mountains, and valleys low,
Through cities bright, and rivers that flow,
With love as our guide, we'll carve our way,
The compass of affection lights our day.

In laughter shared, in silence known,
Together we find our truest home.
For every journey, near or afar,
You are my compass, my guiding star.

Finding Our Way

In the labyrinth of dreams we wander,
Through twists and turns, we pause and ponder.
With every choice, our paths align,
Hand in hand, the stars brightly shine.

Through fog and shadows, we tread with care,
Finding our way in the open air.
With whispered hopes and gentle grace,
In each other's arms, we find our place.

The road ahead may be rough and steep,
But together we promise, our love we'll keep.
Navigating storms, we'll never stray,
Each step with purpose, come what may.

In the light of dawn, new horizons rise,
With every sunrise, our spirits fly.
We carve our story in moments we share,
Finding our way, it's always fair.

With courage as our guiding light,
We face the world, ready to fight.
Together we'll journey, come what may,
In the book of life, we'll find our way.

Serenities of Synergy

In the dance of souls, we intertwine,
Creating harmonies, pure and divine.
Through laughter and silence, we find our tune,
A symphony played beneath the moon.

Two voices mingle in whispers sweet,
Creating magic with each heartbeat.
Synergy born from love's embrace,
In our world together, we find our place.

Like rivers merging, flowing as one,
Our journey together has only begun.
In the stillness, we hear the call,
Creating futures where love conquers all.

With each sunset, our spirits soar,
Exploring the wonders that lie in store.
In collaboration, our hearts connect,
Serenities bloom, a perfect reflect.

Through trials faced, we stand side by side,
In unity's strength, we take our stride.
With every breath, our spirits align,
In the serenity of synergy, you are mine.

The Bridge of Forgiveness

Across the river, shadows play,
Building bridges, come what may.
In silence spoken, hearts can mend,
Forgiveness floats, a gentle bend.

With every step, the weight feels light,
Two souls united in the night.
A whisper soft, we let it be,
Forgiveness thrives, and sets us free.

The past may linger, but we strive,
To forge a path where love will thrive.
In the embrace of tender grace,
We find our peace, in this safe space.

A bridge that sways, yet strong it stands,
Forgiveness nurtured, hand in hand.
The bonds that break begin to heal,
In this soft glow, our truth revealed.

So let us walk, with heads held high,
On this bridge where spirits fly.
With every step, let go the pain,
Forgiveness here, our sweet refrain.

The Flow of Connection

In every look, a story told,
Connections spark, both warm and bold.
Through rivers deep, our spirits flow,
A gentle touch, the seeds we sow.

Through laughter shared, through tears we cry,
We weave a tapestry, you and I.
In moments small, our hearts align,
The flow of connection, pure and divine.

A dance of souls, entwined in fate,
Each heartbeat echoes, never late.
In silence, whispers bridge the gap,
The flow of love, a sacred map.

Through seasons change, we stand as one,
The stream of life, it just begun.
In every pulse, the rhythm sways,
Connection thrives in countless ways.

So let it flow, this sacred art,
Bring love's embrace to every heart.
With open arms, we journey on,
In connection's light, we are reborn.

Threads That Bind

In every stitch, a tale unfolds,
Threads that bind in colors bold.
Woven tightly, side by side,
In this fabric, we confide.

The golden threads of joy and pain,
Embroidered hearts that will remain.
In every knot, a promise made,
Threads that bind will never fade.

Through laughter's weave and sorrow's seam,
Together we fulfill the dream.
A tapestry of lives entwined,
The threads that bind, forever kind.

So let us stitch with love and care,
In every moment, truths we share.
With every pull, we grow in kind,
The beauty lies in threads that bind.

As seasons change, our design does too,
In shades of life, both old and new.
These threads unite, through thick and thin,
In every heart, the love within.

The Rhythm of Reciprocity

In every glance, a give and take,
The rhythm flows, for love's own sake.
Two hearts that beat in perfect time,
A dance of souls, a silent rhyme.

The balance keeps us side by side,
With every gesture, hearts open wide.
In giving kindness, we receive,
A cycle pure, we both believe.

With every word, we build anew,
A bridge of trust, between us two.
In rhythm's grace, we find a way,
To honor love, each passing day.

The ebb and flow, like tides of fate,
In harmony, we celebrate.
Through acts of love, we both will see,
The rhythm of sweet reciprocity.

So let us share this dance, my friend,
A journey true, that has no end.
In every heartbeat, let it be,
The rhythm flows, through you and me.

The Dance of Diversities

In hues of laughter, we twirl,
Each difference a petal, a swirl.
With footsteps guided by the sun,
Together we shine, a dance begun.

Melodies blend, a vibrant song,
In every heartbeat, we belong.
Together we weave our stories wide,
In unity's arms, we take pride.

Colors of culture take their stance,
A joyful mix in this lively dance.
We celebrate what makes us real,
In each embrace, a shared ideal.

With open hearts, we step in time,
Our voices rise, a perfect rhyme.
Embracing all that life imparts,
In every beat, the dance of hearts.

As seasons change and moments flow,
Our differences nurture, help us grow.
In every twirl, the world we see,
A beautiful dance, you and me.

Reflections of Togetherness

In shadows cast, reflections glow,
A mirror showing love's warm flow.
Hand in hand, we face the light,
In every heart, our hopes ignite.

Through stormy nights and sunny days,
Together we navigate the maze.
Each whispered word a gentle bond,
In every pause, our hearts respond.

With laughter shared and tears embraced,
In every struggle, we find our place.
A tapestry of souls combined,
In truth and faith, our hearts aligned.

When joys are high and sorrows low,
In this garden, love will grow.
With woven dreams, we lift our song,
In every note, we all belong.

A symphony of vibrant views,
In every path, we choose to choose.
Together we rise, hand in hand,
In reflections clear, we understand.

Riddles of the Heart

In silent whispers, secrets dwell,
The heart holds riddles it will tell.
With each beat, a question sings,
In love's embrace, the mystery clings.

Through veils of doubt, we search for clues,
In tender moments, we choose our views.
With every glance, a puzzle starts,
In quiet depths, we trace our hearts.

The language of the soul unfolds,
In shared glances, the truth beholds.
With every tear and every smile,
The riddles fade, if just a while.

In labyrinths of passion and pain,
We chase the answers, love makes gain.
With open hearts, we dare to trust,
In every journey, find what's just.

The heart's own riddles pull us tight,
Together shining in the night.
In time's embrace, the answer's clear,
In love, the riddles disappear.

The Echoing Embrace

In quiet corners, echoes rise,
A gentle touch, beneath the skies.
With arms wide open, we find a space,
In every heartbeat, the echoing grace.

Through whispered dreams, we softly speak,
In every vow, together seek.
A circle woven with threads of gold,
In different stories, love unfolds.

With memories held in tender light,
We journey far, through day and night.
Each echo tells of paths we've crossed,
In every bond, no love is lost.

In shadows cast, our laughter rings,
Through every moment, the solace brings.
With every hug, a warm embrace,
In unity's fold, we find our place.

As twilight falls, the stars appear,
In the echo of love, we hold dear.
Together we stand, in life's sweet thrum,
In every echo, love will come.

Threads of Intimacy

In quiet moments, hands entwine,
Whispers their secrets, the heart's design.
Soft gazes shared, a silent song,
Two souls in rhythm, where they belong.

A tender touch that speaks of trust,
Memories woven, a bond robust.
Each heartbeat a promise, deep and clear,
In threads of intimacy, love draws near.

Through laughter's echoes and shadows cast,
In woven tales of the days gone past.
Pain and joy, in colors bright,
Together they dance, embracing light.

The fabric of life, stitched with care,
In every smile, a story to share.
In the warmth of a gaze, they find their way,
Threads of intimacy guide their stay.

With every tear, joy's hand wipes dry,
Creating a tapestry that can't deny.
In the loom of love, they find their place,
Forever together, in this sacred space.

Balancing Acts in Love

Two hearts on a wire, a delicate dance,
Finding the rhythm, embracing the chance.
Steps of faith, in unison tread,
With laughter and love, worries shed.

In the push and the pull, they sway and glide,
Life's little moments, they do not hide.
A give and take, a gentle embrace,
In balancing acts, they find their grace.

When storms arise, they hold on tight,
Through the darkness, they search for light.
With patience and care, every fall's a gain,
In the ebb and the flow, they'll break the chain.

Every doubt met with courage anew,
Every challenge, a chance to renew.
Through thick and thin, their love you'll find,
In balancing acts, their hearts aligned.

With dreams intertwined, they dare to aspire,
Building a life that sets the heart afire.
Through trials faced and triumphs shared,
In balancing acts, their souls are bared.

Navigating Emotional Waves

Like tides that rise and fall with grace,
Emotions shift, in the vast space.
Navigating depths where currents flow,
Together they learn, together they grow.

In storms of doubt, they hold the line,
Through crashing waves, their hearts entwine.
Riding the highs, embracing the lows,
In the ocean of love, true wisdom flows.

With each passing crest, they find their way,
Guided by stars, through night and day.
A compass of trust, they steer with heart,
In navigating waves, they choose to start.

As surges fade and calm prevails,
In the stillness, their love unveils.
The journey ahead, an azure sea,
In navigating waves, they're forever free.

Through tears of joy and whispers of pain,
They gather strength, like falling rain.
Together they sail, hand in glove,
Navigating waves, united in love.

Conversations Under Stars

Beneath the vast, twinkling skies,
Whispers of dreams and soft goodbyes.
Stars spell secrets, in twilight's embrace,
In conversations under stars, they find their place.

Voices blend in night's sweet hush,
Time slows down in the gentle rush.
Sharing desires and fears so deep,
In this enchanted hour, their hearts leap.

Stories unfold in the lunar light,
Each word a spark, igniting the night.
With laughter and sighs, the moments spin,
In conversations under stars, their souls begin.

From distant worlds, to the here and now,
Promises made in a solemn vow.
Each twinkle a witness, each sigh a thread,
In the cosmic dance, love is widespread.

As dawn approaches, they hold on tight,
Carrying dreams into morning light.
In the beauty of silence, hearts align,
In conversations under stars, their souls entwine.

Threads of Understanding

In the fabric of thoughts we weave,
Each thread a story to believe.
Colors blend in gentle grace,
Creating bonds we can embrace.

Through dialogue, we learn and grow,
In every word, a seed we sow.
With open hearts, we share the light,
Transforming darkness into bright.

Embrace the differences we find,
A tapestry of heart and mind.
Together strong, we stand as one,
A journey shared, never done.

In the silence, listen close,
To the echoes we cherish most.
Building bridges, understanding,
A future bright, ever expanding.

With every thread, connections made,
A legacy that will not fade.
Together we craft a world so grand,
United, we take a stand.

Whispers Across the Divide

In the gentle breeze, we hear the call,
Whispers rising, bridging all.
Voices soft, yet deeply strong,
Together we find where we belong.

Across the chasm, hearts extend,
Sowing seeds that love will tend.
Building trust with every breath,
Transforming fear, embracing depth.

In the silence, stories flow,
Each tale shared helps us grow.
Fostering kindness, creating peace,
In unity, our fears will cease.

Weaving dreams with threads of hope,
Together we learn to cope.
With open arms, we start anew,
Discovering paths, both bright and true.

So let the whispers guide our way,
Unraveling doubts with each new day.
Hand in hand, we face the rise,
In love's embrace, we'll touch the skies.

Tides of Togetherness

Waves of laughter, rolling free,
Washing shores of you and me.
In the ocean's gentle sway,
We find resilience every day.

The currents pull, yet we hold tight,
Guided by the moonlit night.
With every ebb, a lesson learned,
In every tide, our passion burned.

Navigating this vast expanse,
Together we dive, together we dance.
Through trials faced, we rise and shine,
In the sea of life, your hand in mine.

As storm clouds gather, we'll stand firm,
In the winds of change, we'll not squirm.
Embracing storms, we'll change the weather,
With hearts as one, we'll brave together.

Let the waves sing our sweet refrain,
In unity, we conquer pain.
Together as the tides will flow,
Where love and hope forever grow.

Navigating the Currents

In the river of life, we chart our way,
With dreams as our compass, come what may.
Every bend tells a tale untold,
Together we venture, brave and bold.

In waters calm and tempest tossed,
We'll find the paths, whatever the cost.
Riding the rapids, we learn to steer,
In the heart of darkness, love will clear.

Through the currents, we take our chance,
With every moment, we learn to dance.
Navigating fears, we find our voice,
In unison, we'll make our choice.

With every challenge, we build our strength,
In unity, we go to great lengths.
Through deep waters and shallow streams,
Together we'll realize our dreams.

So let us sail this journey wide,
With open hearts, we'll turn the tide.
Hand in hand, let our spirits soar,
In life's great river, forevermore.

Unwritten Rules of Love

In silence we find what words can't share,
The glances exchanged in the open air.
Each heartbeat drums a familiar beat,
In the shadows, love wakes from its sleep.

Soft whispers weave the fabric tight,
Promises linger in the quiet night.
The distance closes with every sigh,
Unspoken truths make the spirit fly.

Through laughter and tears, we find our way,
Moments cherished, not meant to sway.
Two souls dancing in a tender trance,
In the rhythm of love, we take our chance.

A gentle touch, a knowing glance,
In the chaos, we find our stance.
Together we build a world of grey,
Where colors blend in a bright array.

Though rules may shift, our love stays true,
In the dance of life, just me and you.
With every misstep, we learn and grow,
In the unwritten, our feelings flow.

The Canvas of Companionship

With colors bright, we paint our days,
A canvas wide, in countless ways.
Each stroke a memory, bold and true,
In the art of together, me and you.

Brushes dipped in laughter's hue,
A splash of dreams, a vision new.
In quiet moments, we blend the shades,
As time moves on, the heart cascades.

Layers build with each shared tale,
Though storms may come, our bond won't pale.
We sketch the future, stroke by stroke,
In every canvas, our words evoke.

Lines of patience, hues of trust,
Through every struggle, in love we must.
The masterpiece of the heart unfolds,
With every whisper, our story told.

Together we dream, together we play,
On life's great canvas, we find our way.
With every artwork, our values bloom,
In this companionship, we're free to assume.

Embracing Vulnerability

In the shadows, we dare to stand,
Exposing hearts, hand in hand.
A tender risk, a chance we take,
To find the strength in hearts that break.

Behind the walls, our secrets hide,
With every confession, we open wide.
In quiet moments, we shed our fears,
Allowing love to fill our tears.

With fragile words, we carve our way,
Embracing truths we dare not say.
In this softness, we find our grace,
Two souls bared in a warm embrace.

No armor worn, just honesty,
In every silence, we choose to be.
Though scars may echo the past we know,
In vulnerability, our spirits grow.

We find the strength in being raw,
In the tender space, we find the awe.
With hearts wide open, to dare and trust,
In embracing the truth, we find our must.

Unraveling the Heart's Language

Whispers echo in the still of night,
In every heartbeat, the truth ignites.
A language spoken without a sound,
In the depths of silence, love is found.

Eyes connect with a knowing glance,
In the rhythm of life, we take our chance.
Every sigh carries tales untold,
In this quiet dance, our hearts unfold.

Fingers trace lines of unspoken dreams,
In the crack of daylight, we are extremes.
The softest touch can shatter the dark,
In unravelling layers, we find the spark.

Together we journey the road unknown,
In every heartbeat, we've truly grown.
The language of love, both simple and vast,
In the folds of time, we hold on fast.

Through tangled thoughts, our souls converse,
In every moment, we find our verse.
In the gentle art of what we feel,
Unraveling love, we find what's real.

Under the Same Skies

Under the gentle moon's glow,
We stand together, hand in hand.
Stars whisper secrets, soft and low,
A silent pact, a timeless bond.

With every twinkle, stories weave,
Of dreams shared and hopes confessed.
In this moment, we believe,
Our hearts forever intertwined.

Wind carries laughter, sweet and bright,
As shadows dance beneath the trees.
The world fades, replaced by light,
Together, we create our peace.

In twilight's embrace, we find our way,
Guided by love, we chart our course.
No words are needed; we simply stay,
Under skies that hold us close.

In every sunset, we will meet,
A promise made in colors pure.
With each heartbeat, we are complete,
Together, under skies obscure.

Threads of Common Ground

In the tapestry of life, we weave,
Threads of laughter, hope, and grace.
Each moment shared, we believe,
Forms a bond time can't erase.

Every story, a stitch in time,
In the fabric of our trust.
Through every mountain, every climb,
We gather strength, it's a must.

In shadows cast, we find the light,
With every tear, our hearts entwine.
Together, storms transform to bright,
Creating paths that intertwine.

With open arms, we face the day,
Together, side by side we stand.
In unity, we find our way,
Creating art with every hand.

In the quiet moments shared,
We forge connections deep and true.
With every smile, we are declared,
Two souls united, me and you.

The Fragrance of Togetherness

In gardens lush, our laughter blooms,
Petals soft, where memories lie.
Every moment, sweet perfume,
In the air, our love will fly.

With every breeze that softly sighs,
Nature sings a gentle tune.
In your presence, I realize,
Together, we make hearts attune.

The fragrance wraps us, warm embrace,
Bringing comfort, a cherished blend.
In each glance, I see your grace,
A bond that time cannot bend.

Through seasons' change, we hold our ground,
Roots entangled beneath the earth.
In each heartbeat, true love is found,
Together, we celebrate worth.

As twilight falls, we share the night,
Stars above, our dreams align.
In this moment, everything's right,
The fragrance of us, pure divine.

A Manual for Two

Step one, a smile to light the way,
With simple words that heal the heart.
In laughter shared, we find our play,
Together, we will never part.

Step two, embrace the stormy days,
When clouds gather and skies turn gray.
In unity, we find the ways,
To lift each other, come what may.

Step three, cherish quiet hours,
Where silence speaks, and hearts can rest.
In peaceful moments, love empowers,
Together, we know we are blessed.

Step four, dance beneath the moonlight,
With rhythm that binds our souls in grace.
In every twirl, we take flight,
Together, we find our place.

As we follow this manual, so true,
We carve our path, with love as guide.
In each chapter, there's me and you,
A story written side by side.

Serenade of Shared Dreams

In the twilight's gentle hold,
Whispers of wishes unfold,
Stars ignite in a shared glance,
Hearts engage in a fleeting dance.

Together we chart the skies,
With hopes that lift, that rise,
Each secret a note in our song,
In unity, we both belong.

Through the valleys, deep and wide,
In your hands, I trust, abide,
Woven tales, both old and new,
In this serenade, just us two.

With every dream, a touch, a sigh,
A symphony as we fly high,
In the echoes of laughter clear,
We'll carve a world without fear.

As dawn creeps in, we hold tight,
In the glow of morning light,
Our dreams, like petals, will bloom,
In this love, there's always room.

The Dance of Vulnerability

In the stillness of the night,
We strip away the hidden light,
With trembling hearts, we expose,
In this dance, our true selves pose.

Each step a tremor, soft yet bold,
In the warmth, our stories unfold,
Fear fades, replaced by grace,
As we move in this sacred space.

Through the shadows, we entwine,
Raw and unguarded, you are mine,
In the truth of every glance,
Together, we take a chance.

A rhythm found in soft confessions,
With every sway, there are lessons,
In vulnerability, we breathe,
In this dance, we choose to believe.

As the evening drapes its cloak,
In this dance, love's whispers spoke,
Here, our fears become our grace,
In the light, we find our place.

A Canvas of Compromise

With colors brushed in tender strokes,
We create where silence spoke,
Each hue a tale of our hearts,
In the canvas, love imparts.

Lines may bend, and shadows blend,
In this art, we learn to mend,
From differences, beauty forms,
In the storms, we weather warms.

In the chaos, a pattern grows,
Through patience, our passion flows,
Together, we shape a scene,
In compromise, what might have been.

Each mark a story to embrace,
In our flaws, we find our grace,
With every brush, a gentle spark,
In this journey, we leave our mark.

As the canvas fills with love's hue,
In depths, we find something true,
In the strokes of give and take,
A masterpiece we both will make.

Shadows and Light

In the folds of dusk's embrace,
Shadows play, finding their place,
With each flicker, a story starts,
Light dances, igniting hearts.

Through the cracks, soft glimmers peep,
In the silence, secrets keep,
We wade through darkness, hand in hand,
In this journey, we understand.

The contrast paints our world anew,
In the night, all dreams break through,
With every shadowed, whispered turn,
In the light, we'll brightly burn.

Together, we forge our path clear,
In every color, hope is near,
With the night, we learn to play,
In shadows, light finds its way.

As the sun begins to rise,
We meet the dawn with open eyes,
In shadows and light, we stand tall,
In this dance of life, we embrace all.

Flourishing in Togetherness

In a garden where laughter grows,
Hands entwined in gentle grace,
We water dreams with whispered hopes,
Together, we find our place.

Every step we take as one,
Shadows dance beneath the sun,
In the embrace of unity,
Our hearts beat, never to shun.

Through storms that threaten to divide,
We build our fortress, side by side,
In the tapestry of our days,
Love's colors never collide.

With every challenge that we face,
Each challenge becomes a thrill,
Together we are strong enough,
To climb each daunting hill.

In this life of shared delight,
With you, the world feels bright,
In every moment, hand in hand,
We flourish in this light.

Words Unspoken

In silence, we find our truth,
A glance speaks louder than sound,
Within the quiet, hearts converse,
In stillness, love is found.

With every breath, a story flows,
Emotions wrapped in gentle care,
In the shadows of unspoken thoughts,
We find the strength to share.

The weight of words left unsaid,
Drifts like leaves in autumn's breeze,
Yet when you hold my silent gaze,
My heart whispers with ease.

In the spaces where voices fade,
Our souls dance without refrain,
Each heartbeat echoes what is felt,
A language without a name.

Through the unvoiced paths we walk,
Connected in our silent ways,
In every sigh, a promise lives,
Where love forever stays.

A Tapestry of Care

Threads of kindness weave and twine,
In every gesture, love's design,
The fabric of our shared heartbeats,
Stitched together, pure and fine.

With each interaction, warmth ignites,
In laughter's glow, the spirit lifts,
In moments small, we find our grace,
In giving, we discover gifts.

Colors blend in vibrant hues,
Compassion threads through every seam,
In the tapestry that we create,
We're united in one dream.

A quilt of memories, soft and warm,
Woven through time, love's embrace,
In every stitch, a story lives,
In every thread, a trace.

So let our hearts forever share,
A tapestry of deep, sweet care,
For in this world of highs and lows,
Together, we are rare.

The Equilibrium of Hearts

In the dance of give and take,
We find a balance pure and true,
With every heartbeat, we align,
In the flow of me and you.

Like the tide that ebbs and flows,
Our love maintains a quiet strength,
In harmony, we rise and fall,
In patience, we find our length.

Through the chaos and the calm,
We navigate the river's bend,
In the union of our souls,
Many journeys find an end.

Each joy and sorrow shared as one,
A scale that weighs both joy and pain,
In the equilibrium we build,
A bond where dreams sustain.

So here we stand, in time's embrace,
With hearts aligned and spirits bright,
In the balance of our love,
We shine like stars in night.

The Dance of Hearts

In moonlight's gentle glow, we sway,
With whispered secrets, we find our way.
Each heartbeat echoes in the night,
Two souls entwined, a pure delight.

Step by step, we move in time,
A rhythm soft, a silent rhyme.
The world fades, just you and I,
As stars above begin to sigh.

With every turn, we lose the ground,
In this embrace, pure love is found.
Two hearts in unison, a single beat,
In this dance, we are complete.

Through shadows cast and dreams we weave,
In every glance, the love we leave.
Together in this fleeting space,
We'll find forever in this place.

When the final notes drift away,
In our hearts, the music will stay.
The dance may cease, but not our song,
In each other's arms, we belong.

In Tune with Two

Two voices blend, a perfect pair,
In harmony, we dance through air.
Each note we play, a sweet embrace,
Melodies woven with love and grace.

With laughter bright, the world feels right,
In every moment, pure delight.
Our hearts compose a symphony,
In tune with all that's meant to be.

Through highs and lows, we share this song,
In every beat, we both belong.
Together crafting dreamy lines,
A story written, love defines.

When silence falls, we still can hear,
A whisper of love, forever near.
Our song remains, through day and night,
In tune with two, our hearts take flight.

So let's embrace the music played,
In every moment, love conveyed.
Together, always we will soar,
In tune with two, forevermore.

The Symphony of Us

In the quiet dawn, we rise and shine,
Two notes collide, a love divine.
With every heartbeat, we play our tune,
Beneath the sun, beneath the moon.

The world may spin, yet we stand still,
In this embrace, we find our thrill.
Each moment shared, a chorus sung,
In perfect harmony, we're forever young.

Through trials faced, our strength revealed,
In every tear, our hearts are healed.
Together, we craft a sweet refrain,
In every joy, and through the pain.

With every laugh, a string we pluck,
Binding our souls, we share our luck.
A symphony of dreams we chase,
In every note, we find our place.

As music swells and fades away,
Our love remains, come what may.
The symphony of us, sweet and grand,
In every heartbeat, hand in hand.

Weaving Connections

In threads of gold, our stories blend,
Weaving connections that never end.
Each moment shared, a tapestry bright,
Crafted together, our hearts take flight.

With every smile, a stitch we find,
Creating pieces that intertwine.
In laughter shared, the colors gleam,
Together we chase the shared dream.

Through trials faced, the fabric strong,
In each other's arms, we both belong.
The heartstrings pull and gently sway,
In this dance, we find our way.

With every tear, we sew anew,
Embracing every shade and hue.
Connections deepen, bonds entwine,
In every heartbeat, love will shine.

As seasons change and threads unwind,
We'll weave our story, love defined.
In this rich tapestry, we find grace,
Weaving connections, we embrace.

Bridges Over Silence

In the stillness, whispers flow,
Connecting hearts, a subtle glow.
Bridges form where silence breaks,
A dance of thoughts, the risk it takes.

Voices echo in the night,
Lifting spirits, taking flight.
Through the gaps, we find our way,
Building bonds that dare to stay.

The shadows talk, the light replies,
In every pause, a truth lies.
Beyond the quiet, we emerge,
In harmony, our passions surge.

Bridges span the endless sea,
Uniting souls in mystery.
In the silence, we ignite,
A spark that turns the dark to light.

So let's embrace the space between,
For in that silence, we are seen.
Forging ties, strong and true,
Bridges built from me and you.

The Language of Love

Softest glances, tender sighs,
In every heartbeat, a surprise.
Words unspoken, yet so clear,
A silent vow, forever near.

In the moonlight, shadows play,
Every moment, love's ballet.
Laughter dances, soft and bright,
In the stillness of the night.

Each touch a promise, warm embrace,
Time stands still in this sacred space.
Language formed without a word,
A symphony that's ever heard.

Through the storms and gentle rain,
Love's warmth will ever remain.
In the silence, echoes blend,
A story woven without end.

The language spoken, heart to heart,
Crafting worlds, we play our part.
Together, forever, side by side,
In love's sweet arms, our souls abide.

Painting with Emotions

Colors splash across the canvas,
Shades of laughter, hues of sadness.
Each stroke a feeling, raw and true,
Life's palette mixed with shades of you.

Brush in hand, the heart's release,
Creating beauty, finding peace.
The canvas whispers secrets old,
Through every color, stories told.

Blue for sorrow, red for fire,
Yellow dreams, and green desire.
A tapestry of life unfolds,
In every stroke, the truth beholds.

With gentle touch, the moment's caught,
Every emotion, a lesson taught.
Painting visions where hearts align,
Crafting memories, purely divine.

So let the colors freely flow,
In every heartbeat, let love grow.
Artful gestures, bold and bright,
Painting our lives, a beautiful sight.

The Alchemy of Us

In the crucible of time and space,
Two souls unite, a sweet embrace.
Transforming shadows into light,
The alchemy of love ignites.

Gold from struggles, silver from tears,
A journey forged through hopes and fears.
Each moment crafted, pure and clear,
In the furnace, we persevere.

Together we dance, a mystic thread,
Weaving futures where dreams are fed.
With every heartbeat, magic flows,
In the rhythm, our passion grows.

From humble elements, we create,
A legacy that won't abate.
In the alchemy, we find our core,
Burning bright, forevermore.

So let us toast to this fine blend,
In love's embrace, we shall transcend.
For in this magic, we are fused,
The alchemy of us, forever used.

Twists and Turns of Trust

In the shadows, whispers creep,
Promises made, secrets to keep.
Hearts entwined, yet doubts arise,
A fragile bond beneath the skies.

Paths diverge on this winding road,
Trust is heavy, a precious load.
Yet hope ignites in tiny sparks,
To guide us through the hidden dark.

In every turn, a lesson learned,
Each misstep, a flame discerned.
With every fall, we rise anew,
Rebuilding trust, a stronger view.

Promises like fragile glass,
They can shatter, they can pass.
But with care, they may restore,
A bond that holds forevermore.

So let us walk this path with grace,
Through twists and turns, we find our place.
With every heartbeat, we hold tight,
Trust can flourish in the night.

The Stillness Within the Storm

Amidst the chaos, silence speaks,
A gentle whisper, a heart that seeks.
In raging winds, a peace can bloom,
A quiet strength against the gloom.

Dark clouds gather, the sky grows gray,
Yet within, there's a brighter way.
Beneath the thunder, hear the calm,
A soothing presence like a balm.

Raindrops dance on the windowpane,
Nature's rhythm, a soft refrain.
In every storm, there lies a chance,
To find the stillness, join the dance.

Embrace the turmoil, let it flow,
For after storms, the flowers grow.
In pain and struggle, strength is found,
In the silent depths, we stand our ground.

So when the tempests loudly call,
Remember stillness can enthrall.
Within the storm, seek peace anew,
And let its might reveal the true.

Fragments of Forever

In fleeting moments, time stands still,
Echoes linger, a heart to fill.
Each fragment sparkles, a memory's grace,
A piece of forever in time and space.

From laughter shared to silent tears,
Every fragment holds our years.
Captured whispers of love's embrace,
Forever etched, they leave a trace.

In photographs and dreams unspooled,
A tapestry of life, beautifully pooled.
Each thread a story, woven tight,
Fragments shine, they hold the light.

In separation, we still connect,
Bound by moments we can reflect.
For in each fragment, a truth is found,
A promise echoes, a love unbound.

Though time may pass and seasons change,
These fragments remain, forever strange.
In the heart's attic, memories soar,
Fragments of forever, always more.

The Palette of Emotion

Colors dancing on the canvas bright,
Each stroke whispers feelings in flight.
From joy to sorrow, hues blend and swirl,
In the palette of emotion, dreams unfurl.

Crimson blushes of love so bold,
Golden passions, stories told.
Cerulean blues of deep despair,
Swirling together, dreams laid bare.

Emerald greens of hope's embrace,
Nature's canvas, a sacred place.
Violet whispers of calm and peace,
In each color, emotions release.

Patterns woven with tender care,
A tapestry of feelings laid bare.
In every shade, a story flows,
The palette of emotion, beauty glows.

So let us paint with vibrant hearts,
Embrace the colors, and play our parts.
In this masterpiece, we find our way,
The palette of emotion lights our day.

Conversations in the Dark

Whispers float on midnight air,
Secrets shared without a care.
Shadows dance in candle's glow,
Hearts reveal what they won't show.

Silence speaks, a soothing balm,
In dark, the souls can find their calm.
Thoughts like stars in velvet sky,
In the dark, we learn to fly.

Voices blend in hushed embrace,
In the stillness, find our place.
Words are cloaked in gentle hue,
Conversations pure and true.

Breaths are soft, the night is deep,
In this space, our dreams we keep.
Time suspended, moments freeze,
In the dark, we're truly free.

With every sigh, the night unfolds,
Stories shared, and truths retold.
In the dark, we shed our light,
Conversations hold us tight.

The Sculpting of Unity

Hands entwined, a dream is born,
Molding hope, a world reborn.
With every touch, we shape our fate,
In this bond, we cultivate.

Voices rise, a chorus strong,
In unity, we all belong.
Each heartbeat echoes pure intent,
Our spirit shines, a firmament.

Together we stand, side by side,
In the storm, we shall abide.
Every clash, a lesson learned,
In the fire, our passion burned.

Through trials faced, our hearts align,
In the struggle, we will shine.
With every step, we forge the way,
In unity, we find our play.

Crafting dreams with hands of grace,
In this dance, we find our place.
As one we rise, as one we sing,
The sculpting of our offering.

Mosaic of Many

Fragments scattered, colors blend,
Each piece tells a tale, a trend.
In diversity, there's strength found,
A mosaic thrives, all around.

Hearts of different hues unite,
Together we shine ever bright.
In the patterns we create,
Each story shares a common fate.

With every shard, a vision grows,
In every crack, a wisdom flows.
Through the gaps, love weaves its thread,
In this tapestry, we are led.

Beauty blooms where scars reside,
In our flaws, we take pride.
A landscape rich with tales untold,
Mosaic hearts that won't grow cold.

Unity in differences shines,
In this dance, our spirit twines.
Together we make a masterpiece,
A mosaic of love that won't cease.

The Wildflower Effect

In the cracks, a bloom appears,
Spreading joy, it calms our fears.
Nature's brush paints hues so bright,
Wildflowers dance in morning light.

Unfettered by the rigid rules,
They thrive where others are mere fools.
With every petal, a story grows,
In their wake, a beauty flows.

Rooted deep but free to sway,
In wildness, they find their way.
A lesson learned from gentle seeds,
In the wild, we find our needs.

Graceful in their chaos found,
They whisper truths, profound.
In resilience, love's pure breath,
Blooms arise, defying death.

Just like them, we too can rise,
In the sun, beneath the skies.
With courage held and hearts so vast,
We sow our love, a wildflower cast.

Harmony in Dissonance

In shadows cast by brightened lights,
We dance along the edge of night.
With every note, a clash and blend,
A melody that has no end.

Through tangled chords, we find our sound,
In chaos, beauty can abound.
Embracing all that feels out of place,
We weave together, interlace.

Each voice distinct, yet harmonized,
Together forged, we are advised.
Within the noise, we write our song,
In disarray, we still belong.

The heartbeats sync, a pulse so true,
Creating art from me and you.
In dissonance, we find our peace,
A shared resonance that won't cease.

Through fractured paths, we journey wide,
With open arms, and hearts as guide.
In every clash, the truth we glean,
Harmony blooms from what has been.

Unraveling the Knots

Life's tangled threads, each weave unique,
In time we see what we must seek.
With gentle hands, we pull and pry,
Letting go, we learn to fly.

Twists of fate can bind us tight,
Yet through the dark, we find our light.
Each struggle, lesson folded small,
With every knot, we rise or fall.

The burdens heavy on our backs,
Lead us to find the hidden tracks.
With patience taught through pain and strife,
We find our way back to real life.

Threads of sorrow, threads of cheer,
Together weave a tapestry here.
Through every pull, a tale is spun,
In unraveling, we find our one.

So take a breath, and slow the pace,
Embrace the journey, every trace.
From frayed to fine, we shall become,
The work of art, the beating drum.

Echoes of Empathy

In quiet moments, hearts will share,
The whispers soft, a tender care.
We resonate, like stones in stream,
Reflecting lives, a shared dream.

With every heartbeat, we connect,
In shared joys or grief, respect.
A silent nod, a knowing glance,
In empathy, we take our stance.

Each story told, a sacred bond,
In trials faced, we grow beyond.
The echoes linger, truths unfold,
In gentle kindness, we are bold.

Through tears and laughter, side by side,
In differences, our souls abide.
We stand as one, through thick and thin,
With open hearts, we let love in.

In every voice, a song to sing,
Compassion blooms, the heart takes wing.
The echoes whisper, loud and clear,
In empathy, we draw near.

Balancing the Scales

In life's great dance, we weigh and measure,
Finding balance is our treasure.
The highs and lows, a careful tread,
Embracing all, we forge ahead.

Through turmoil faced, we seek the calm,
In chaos found, we find our balm.
With every choice, a path to find,
We mold our fate, our hearts aligned.

The scales can tip, yet still we stand,
In unity, our hearts expand.
For every loss, a lesson gained,
In each decision, wisdom's trained.

A heartbeat here, a heartbeat there,
In moments shared, we show we care.
Through balance sought, we learn to yield,
In every challenge, love is revealed.

So walk with grace, and choose with heart,
For in these scales, we play our part.
With open arms and hearts so wide,
Together, we will turn the tide.

Unspoken Promises

In the silence we find our grace,
Words unvoiced, yet hearts embrace.
Fingers intertwined, dreams take flight,
Bound by love, we chase the light.

Secrets linger in the air,
Whispers soft, a tender care.
Time stands still, moments freeze,
In your eyes, my heart finds ease.

Promises woven, strong yet slight,
In the dark, we seek the bright.
Each heartbeat echoes, sweet refrain,
In this dance, we feel no pain.

Through the storms and endless night,
Together we reach for the height.
Silent vows, forever stay,
Unspoken love leads the way.

In every glance, a story told,
A warmth that never grows old.
With unspoken dreams we rise,
In each other, we find the skies.

A Symphony of Souls

In the twilight, hearts align,
A melody, sweet and divine.
Strings of fate, intertwined,
In harmony, our spirits bind.

Notes of laughter, echoes clear,
In this song, we conquer fear.
Rhythms dance in moonlight's glow,
A symphony only we know.

Voices blend in soft embrace,
Carving time, a sacred space.
With every beat, the world ignites,
In our union, love ignites.

When the silence dares to creep,
We find strength, our dreams we keep.
In every note, a promise stays,
In this symphony, our hearts blaze.

Together we're a timeless song,
In every chord, where we belong.
A masterpiece of souls entwined,
In this music, love defined.

Reflections in the Mirror

Glimpses of who we used to be,
Haunting images, wild and free.
In the glass, a tale unfolds,
Of whispered secrets, dreams untold.

Shadows flicker, memories play,
Each reflection leads the way.
Fragments of life, moments survive,
In our hearts, the past is alive.

With every tear and joyous laugh,
The mirror shows a crafted path.
Looking closer, we start to see,
The beauty in our history.

Time won't fade the love we share,
In every glance, we find our care.
Reflections in the silent night,
Guide us toward the morning light.

In that glass, we find our strength,
Holding tightly, we go the length.
Through the years, our spirits soar,
In reflections, we find more.

Roots and Wings

Deep in the soil, our roots entwine,
Nurtured by love, a bond defined.
Through storms we stand, steadfast and bold,
In each other, we find our hold.

With every challenge, we grow tall,
Branches reaching, we heed the call.
Wings unfurl, we seek the skies,
Together we rise, our spirits fly.

From the earth, we draw our power,
In the sun, our dreams devour.
Grounded firm, yet freely roam,
In this journey, we find our home.

In every heartbeat, strength remains,
We weather life's unyielding rains.
Roots and wings, forever blend,
In our hearts, we transcend.

With love as our compass, we explore,
Through every door, we seek more.
Boundless paths and endless views,
Together, we paint life's hues.

Underneath the Surface

In shadows deep where whispers lie,
The secrets held, no need to cry.
A world unseen, yet full of grace,
We search for truth in hidden space.

Beneath the waves, a heart beats slow,
The currents pull, yet love will glow.
In silence speaks the loudest voice,
A tender hope, a quiet choice.

Roots intertwined beneath the ground,
A bond created, love profound.
Through cracks and crevices we heal,
The strength of love is what we feel.

Beneath the surface, life takes hold,
Each story shared, more precious than gold.
With every pulse, we find our way,
In this deep world, together we stay.

Though hidden depths may seem so far,
Our hearts align like the morning star.
In murky waters, we learn to swim,
Together facing all that's dim.

The Tapestry of Us

Threads of joy and strands of pain,
Weaving life through sun and rain.
Each stitch a moment we hold tight,
Creating warmth that glows at night.

Colors blend in vibrant hues,
The stories told in countless views.
From laughter shared to tears we've shed,
A tapestry of love is spread.

With every twist, the fabric bends,
In gentle ways, the journey sends.
A bond that's formed with each encounter,
In every heart, a love that's about to mount here.

As seasons change, we keep on weaving,
Through joyful days and nights believing.
No single thread is ever lost,
Together, we embrace the cost.

In this design, we find our way,
Every challenge becomes a play.
A tapestry that tells our tale,
In unity, we will prevail.

The Colors of Commitment

In shades of blue, our dreams take flight,
With every promise, hearts unite.
The canvas broad, we paint with care,
A vibrant life we choose to share.

The reds of passion, burning bright,
The greens of growth, a pure delight.
In softer shades of tender grace,
We find our love in every space.

Through storms and sun, our colors blend,
In every twist, a faithful friend.
The hues of laughter, the strokes of tears,
We paint our future, conquer fears.

With every layer, we define,
The richness of this life, divine.
A masterpiece that will endure,
When colors merge, we're ever sure.

In this artwork, we find our way,
Each brush of fate, a bright display.
The colors spark a flame so grand,
In commitment's dance, we take a stand.

Balmy Breezes of Belonging

The whispers of the evening breeze,
Carry stories through the trees.
In every gust, a tender sigh,
A sense of home, where hearts fly high.

Along the shore, our footprints trace,
In sandy paths, we find our place.
The waves serenade a gentle tune,
Beneath the stars, we find our boon.

With twilight's glow, our fears unwind,
In shared laughter, solace we find.
Every moment, a breath of peace,
In balmy nights, our doubts release.

Together we dance in the soft moonlight,
Embracing dreams that feel so right.
In every heartbeat, love's sweet song,
In balmy breezes, we belong.

As seasons drift, our roots grow deep,
In memories shared, our bonds we keep.
The warmth of belonging never fades,
In every heart, a memory cascades.

Crescendo of Connection

In whispers shared beneath the stars,
Hearts intertwine, erasing scars.
Through laughter's lift and silent tears,
A bond grows stronger over the years.

Voices blend in harmony sweet,
Every moment, a rhythmic beat.
With every glance, a spark ignites,
Creating warmth on wintry nights.

Hands held tight, we brave the storm,
Finding solace in each other's form.
Through shadows cast, we'll find our way,
A brighter dawn, a new day's play.

Together we rise, never apart,
A symphony played, two beating hearts.
In the echo of dreams, we align,
Creating a world that's yours and mine.

Crescendo builds, the world in sight,
With every breath, we chase the light.
In unity, we'll face life's dance,
Bound by love and fate's sweet chance.

The Strength in Softness

A gentle touch can break the stone,
In quiet strength, love is shown.
In tender gestures, power lies,
Soft whispers hold the wisest ties.

The brave expose their fragile side,
In vulnerability, fears subside.
With hearts unveiled, we find our might,
In the warmth of kindness, we ignite.

Through storms that rage and winds that howl,
Let softness guide; let kindness prowl.
A calming presence in the fray,
Brings solace to the harshest day.

In the art of gentle ways we thrive,
A vibrant spirit, alive, alive!
With every hug, a fortress grows,
Wrapped in love, the inner glow shows.

Softness is strength, a paradox true,
In softest whispers, we find the new.
Together we stand, hand in hand,
In strength and softness, we make our stand.

Navigating the Unseen

Through shadows deep where silence dwells,
We seek the truth that whisper tells.
In the depths of night, we wander slow,
Finding paths where moonlight glows.

The heart's compass, a guiding light,
Leads us through the darkest night.
With intuition, we gauge the way,
Trusting the signs that softly sway.

In the quiet hum of the unknown,
Strength is found when we're alone.
With courage wrapped in gentle grace,
We face the world, we find our place.

Navigating dreams and doubts that stream,
We harvest hope from the unseen.
Through tangled thoughts, we carve our way,
A journey forged in night and day.

With every step, we learn to see,
The beauty hidden, wild, and free.
In echoes soft, we shall be whole,
Navigating life with a brave soul.

Mirroring Each Other

In your eyes, I see my dreams,
Reflecting hopes like sunlight beams.
Every laugh, a shared delight,
In mirrored moments, pure and bright.

We dance in sync through joys and pain,
Finding comfort in the rain.
Your heartbeat sings the same sweet tune,
Beneath the watchful, silver moon.

In every glance, a story told,
Through whispered secrets, hearts unfold.
Each challenge faced, we meet as one,
Together shining like the sun.

In the silence, our souls entwine,
A reflection of the divine.
With every step, we learn and grow,
Mirroring love in the ebb and flow.

Together we rise, hand in hand,
In the mirror of love, we stand.
Through all of life's embrace and burden,
We find our strength in this sweet garden.

Seasons of Togetherness

In springtime bloom, our laughter flies,
Underneath the bright, azure skies.
Nature's canvas, colors blend,
Every moment, hand in hand we spend.

Summer's warmth embraces tight,
Sunset whispers, cherished night.
Fingers tracing warmth on skin,
In this season, love begins.

Autumn leaves, a golden dance,
In every step, we find romance.
Crisp air carries stories old,
Wrapped in smiles, together bold.

Winter's chill draws hearts near,
Fireside shadows, our laughter clear.
With cozy nights and dreams untold,
In every chill, our warmth unfolds.

Through seasons' change, we build our song,
In every note, where we belong.
Together, we weather the storms we see,
In the seasons of love, just you and me.

Choreography of Affection

With every glance, a subtle sway,
Our hearts find rhythm, come what may.
In gentle whispers, hope ignites,
Our dances blend under moonlit nights.

Fingers twirl in perfect sync,
Lost in starlight, we will not blink.
With every spin, passion grows,
An artful language only we know.

Together we leap, and together we fall,
In the silence, we hear love's call.
Our shadows merge in a graceful glide,
In this choreography, we confide.

Through the laughter and the tears,
We create a ballet throughout the years.
With each movement, a promise made,
In this duet, our love won't fade.

As time unfolds our story well,
In every note, our hearts will dwell.
In the dance of life, forever we're free,
Choreographed by love's decree.

The Weaving of Us

Threads of gold in every glance,
In every moment, we find our dance.
Stitching dreams with laughter's thread,
In the tapestry of life, we're led.

Fabric soft, with colors bright,
We create warmth in the coldest night.
Sewing memories, side by side,
With every stitch, our hearts confide.

In patterns deep, our souls are spun,
Together, we rise, like the morning sun.
Every knot tied with care and love,
A gift from the universe above.

The weaving grows with time and grace,
In every fold, a sacred space.
With threads interlaced, the stories yield,
In this fabric of us, our hearts are healed.

As the years pass, our quilt unfolds,
A masterpiece, rich and bold.
In colors and textures, forever we trust,
In the weaving of us, a bond so robust.

Paths of Intimacy

On winding trails, our footsteps blend,
Through whispered secrets, love transcends.
In every pause, a chance to share,
In the soft glow, we lay ourselves bare.

Beneath the stars, our dreams collide,
In quiet moments, we confide.
With gentle words and tender sighs,
Our hearts unfold beneath the skies.

Each path we tread, a new embrace,
Every heartbeat finds its place.
In the silence, our souls ignite,
In the dance of shadows, we take flight.

Through time and space, we roam and explore,
In the places where love restores.
Hand in hand, through thick and thin,
In these paths of intimacy, we win.

As the journey winds, our love grows strong,
In every step, we each belong.
Together forever, come what may,
On paths of intimacy, we will stay.

Unwinding the Thread

In shadows deep, the thread unwinds,
A gentle pull, time softly binds.
Each twist a tale, each knot a sigh,
We weave our dreams, then watch them fly.

Fingers dance on fabric worn,
Each stitch a memory, lightly torn.
With every stroke, we seek to mend,
The tapestry that will not end.

Bright colors fade, yet some remain,
In moments lost, in echoes' gain.
The loom of life, it turns so slow,
Yet in its grace, our spirits grow.

As threads entwine, a story grows,
In silent whispers, heartbeats flow.
We find our way through threads of light,
Unwinding dreams into the night.

The final weave, a work of art,
Each frayed edge speaks of a heart.
As dawn breaks through the darkened thread,
A new beginning, gently spread.

The Cycle of Understanding

In circles drawn, the paths align,
We journey forth, through space and time.
Each heart a compass, guiding true,
In every lesson, something new.

With open minds, we seek to hear,
The stories shared, both far and near.
In silence held, and words exchanged,
We find the bonds that once seemed strange.

The rhythm flows like rivers wide,
A cycle spun, where love can't hide.
In giving trust, we learn to grow,
Embracing all, both high and low.

As seasons change, so do our views,
We find the light in others' shoes.
In every step, a bridge we build,
With every heart, the world fulfilled.

In unity, we break the wall,
A tapestry where we stand tall.
For every heartbeat, every sigh,
In understanding, we learn to fly.

Parley of Hearts

In gentle whispers, hearts convene,
A soulful dance, serene yet keen.
Each word a touch, a spark of fire,
In the parley of dreams, we share desire.

Two souls entwined, like vines that grow,
In fragrant air, our passions flow.
The cadence of laughter fills the void,
A connection forged, never destroyed.

With every glance, a story stirs,
In tender silence, love concurs.
Each heartbeat sings a sweet refrain,
In this union, no fear of pain.

Through trials faced and joys that soar,
In trust, we find what hearts adore.
Together we stand, against the tide,
In the parley of hearts, side by side.

For in this meeting, worlds align,
A sacred bond, a love divine.
With every word, the magic grows,
In the parley of hearts, love flows.

The Fire of Connection

A flicker dims, then bursts to flame,
In sharing thoughts, we play the game.
Each ember glows with stories bold,
A fire kindled, warmth to hold.

Through sparks ignited, spirits rise,
In laughter bright, our joy complies.
The flames dance high, a vibrant scene,
In the heart's hearth, love must convene.

With open arms, we draw near,
In the glow, we face our fear.
For deep connections light the way,
Burning brightly, night and day.

As shadows flicker, truth reveals,
The warmth of kindred spirit feels.
In every bond, a legacy stone,
With every flame, we are not alone.

As embers fade, new fires ignite,
In shared moments, our souls take flight.
The fire of connection forever seen,
A beacon bright, where love has been.

Temptations of Trust

In shadows deep, the whispers play,
A dance of doubt in light of day.
The heart's soft plea, a fragile song,
Yet trust, it weaves where we belong.

A gaze so sweet, a sweet deceit,
Every promise, a bittersweet treat.
We long for truth in silent nights,
Temptation's grip, it holds so tight.

Threads of hope, through fingers slip,
As dreams unwind, we lose our grip.
Yet in the dark, a flicker glows,
The trust we mend, the path we choose.

With every fall, we learn to rise,
In fragile bonds, our spirit flies.
To trust again, a daunting feat,
Yet love beckons, its pulse discreet.

In every doubt, there lies a spark,
The flame of faith ignites the dark.
Temptations come and go in time,
But trust, once forged, can truly shine.

The Garden of Us

In a bloom of colors, hearts entwine,
A vivid canvas, your hand in mine.
Each petal soft, a promise shared,
In fragrant whispers, the world is bared.

Beneath the sky, where hopes ascend,
A tapestry woven, love won't bend.
Through seasons change, our roots hold tight,
In storms we'll dance, in sun we'll write.

A quiet pond reflects our dreams,
In gentle ripples, our laughter beams.
Together we grow, two souls as one,
A serenade beneath the sun.

With every seed, a memory sown,
In the garden of us, we've brightly grown.
Through thorns and trials, we dare to trust,
In the arms of love, we bloom robust.

So take my hand in this garden wide,
With you beside me, I feel alive.
Let every flower tell our tale,
In the garden of us, we shall not fail.

Heartstrings and Harmonies

In the silence, our hearts compose,
A symphony where kindness flows.
Every glance, a note we play,
In tunes of love, we find our way.

With every laugh, a chorus rings,
In whispers soft, the soul takes wings.
We chase the dreams in perfect tune,
As stars above begin to croon.

Through seasons' dance, our melody grows,
In the ebb and flow, the sweetness glows.
Each heartbeat sings in vibrant hue,
In harmonies rich, it's me and you.

In the stillness, when shadows creep,
Our song remains, a promise to keep.
Through high and low, our spirits soar,
Together, forever, we'll crave for more.

So let the world hear our refrain,
In love's embrace, through joy and pain.
For every heart, in truth, shall know,
The beauty found when we let go.

The Balance of Being

In the dance of life, we find our grace,
With every challenge, we embrace.
A gentle sway, both near and far,
In balance held, like sun and star.

Through highs and lows, we learn to walk,
In silence deep, we start to talk.
Each moment sweet, a fragile thread,
We weave our paths where fears are shed.

With every breath, the whispers guide,
In stillness, chaos starts to hide.
A mindful pause, a chance to see,
The dance within, the balance of being.

We rise and fall, like ocean's tide,
In ebb and flow, we must abide.
For every storm, there comes a peace,
In balance found, our souls find release.

So trust the journey, let it unfold,
In stories rich, and wisdom bold.
For in the heart, a truth we seek,
The balance of being makes us unique.

The Art of Understanding

To see the world through another's eyes,
To listen close with open hearts and minds.
In silence shared, compassion lies,
A bridge of thought where kindness finds.

Words may falter, but gestures speak,
In empathy, a path revealed.
The strength to listen is what we seek,
In every soul, a story concealed.

A gentle touch, a knowing glance,
Unfolds the layers of one's pain.
In moments shared, we find the chance,
To heal the heart and break the chain.

In every difference, beauty blooms,
Like flowers dancing in the sun.
In understanding, our heart consumes,
The art of love has just begun.

So let us cherish what we find,
In every tale, both dark and bright.
For in the dance of heart and mind,
We forge a future wrapped in light.

Bridges of Trust

In whispers soft, connections grow,
With every promise, a seed is sown.
Through trials faced and storms that blow,
The bonds we build can be our own.

Honesty is the sturdy plank,
That spans the chasm of our fears.
In vulnerability, we thank,
The strength to share both laughs and tears.

A quiet word can soothe the soul,
While actions taken show we care.
Together we can reach the goal,
On pathways paved by trust we share.

In every smile, a hint of grace,
A light of hope when shadows loom.
Through every challenge that we face,
We weave a tapestry to bloom.

So let us walk this road as one,
With faith in hearts and hands held tight.
For bridges formed in love will run,
Beyond the limits of our sight.

Harmony in Dissonance

In chords that clash, a tune may rise,
In every note, a story told.
Through chaos found, a beauty lies,
Where hearts entwine, both brave and bold.

The contrast sharp can spark a flame,
A dance of rhythms, fierce and sweet.
In disarray, we find a name,
For every song that stirs our feet.

When voices blend and clash alike,
We celebrate the push and pull.
With every sound, a chance to hike,
The paths we walk, though often dull.

In mismatched beats, a truth will flow,
Like rivers carving through the stone.
In every discord, let us grow,
For harmony is not alone.

So here's to tones that might be strange,
To melodies that find their way.
Through dissonance, the heart can change,
And sing a song of brighter day.

Echoes of Shared Moments

In laughter shared beneath the stars,
In whispers soft, the world stands still.
Time weaves its patterns, though we are far,
Those echoes linger, sweet and shrill.

A fleeting glance, a fleeting smile,
Moments captured, forever dear.
Through distance, love can bridge each mile,
And memories make the heart clear.

Life's tapestry is sewn with care,
Each thread a story of you and me.
In every breath, in every prayer,
A bond that's stitched in harmony.

With every touch, with every glance,
The world expands, and hopes take flight.
In shared embrace, we find our dance,
Through echoes that still feel so right.

So let us cherish what has been,
The moments that define our way.
For in our hearts, they shall not thin,
The echoes of love will always stay.

Milton Keynes UK
Ingram Content Group UK Ltd.
UKHW021914281024
450365UK00017B/796